W9-DED-500

1100 1200 1300 1400 1500 1600 1700 1800 1900 2000

CANADA THROUGH TIME

Immigration
and the
Founding of
New Communities

Kathleen Corrigan

capstone

Read Me is published by Heinemann Raintree,
an imprint of Capstone Press,
1710 Roe Crest Drive, North Mankato, Minnesota 56003

© 2016 Heinemann-Raintree
an imprint of Capstone Global Library, LLC
Chicago, Illinois

To contact Capstone please visit www.mycapstone.com

Edited by James Benefield
Designed by Philippa Jenkins
Original illustrations © Capstone Global Library Ltd 2016
Picture research by Kelly Garvin
Production by Victoria Fitzgerald
Originated by Capstone Global Library Limited
Printed and bound in China

ISBN 978 1 410 98121 9 (hardback)
19 18 17 16 15
10 9 8 7 6 5 4 3 2 1

ISBN 978 1 410 98126 4 (paperback)
19 18 17 16 15
10 9 8 7 6 5 4 3 2 1

ISBN 978 1 410 98131 8 (ebook)

Acknowledgments
Photo credits: Alamy: Chronicle, 15, Homer Skyes, 22; Capstone Studio/Karon Dubke, 29; Corbis: American Museum of Natural History/National Geographic Creative, 18, Hulton-Deutsch Collection, 26, John E. Marriott, 23, Stefano Bianchetti, 13; Getty Images: Ann Ronan Pictures/Print Collector, 16, Apic, cover (bottom), Hulton Archive, 12, LL/Roger Viollet, 24; Granger, NYC, 25; Library and Archives Canada: Acc.No. 1991-274-2, 7, C-036153, 17, Canada Dept. of the Interior collection, PA-041367, 5, PA-038703, 19, PA- 066544, 11, PA-088504, cover (top), R231-1923-9-E, 8, S.J. Thompson, PA-051372, 21, The Carbon Studio, PA-164916, 27; North Wind Picture Archives, 14; Shutterstock: Darren Baker, 10, David Bukach, 6, Eugene Sergeev, 20, Family Business, 28, Phil McDonald, 9.

Every effort has been made to contact copyright holders of any material reproduced in this book. Any omissions will be rectified in subsequent printings if notice is given to the publisher.

All the Internet addresses (URLs) given in this book were valid at the time of going to press. However, due to the dynamic nature of the Internet, some addresses may have changed, or sites may have changed or ceased to exist since publication. While the author and publisher regret any inconvenience this may cause readers, no responsibility for any such changes can be accepted by either the author or the publisher.

Some words are shown in bold, **like this.** You can find out what they mean by looking in the glossary.

Contents

A new country

In 1867, a group of British **colonies** in North America formed a new country. It was called Canada. Soon after, other **provinces** and **territories** joined too. However, many parts of central and western Canada had few **settlers**. Soon Canadians and new people from Europe began to look there for free land.

Map of Canada around 1885.

Northwest Territories

Keewatin

British Columbia

District of Athabasca

Newfoundland

District of Saskatchewan

Québec

District of Assiniboia

Manitoba

Ontario

Nova Scotia

Disputed area

United States

Many **Aboriginal** people were already living on land the settlers wanted.

The prairies

The Canadian government wanted more **settlers** – the prairies had land that could be farmed. New farms would bring more money into Canada. The government made **treaties** with the Plains **First Nations**. The treaties made some land available for **immigrants**.

The prairies had many hectares of open land for farming.

DID YOU KNOW?

The treaties gave the First Nations people money, blankets, tools, and farm supplies. Yet they took away their land and made them live on reserves.

The North West Mounted Police

American traders wanted to sell things in western Canada. However, they fought with some **First Nations** people. In 1873, the Canadian government started a police force to stop trouble. The force was called the North West Mounted Police.

Mounted police helped protect many Canadians, including First Nations people, traders, and railway builders.

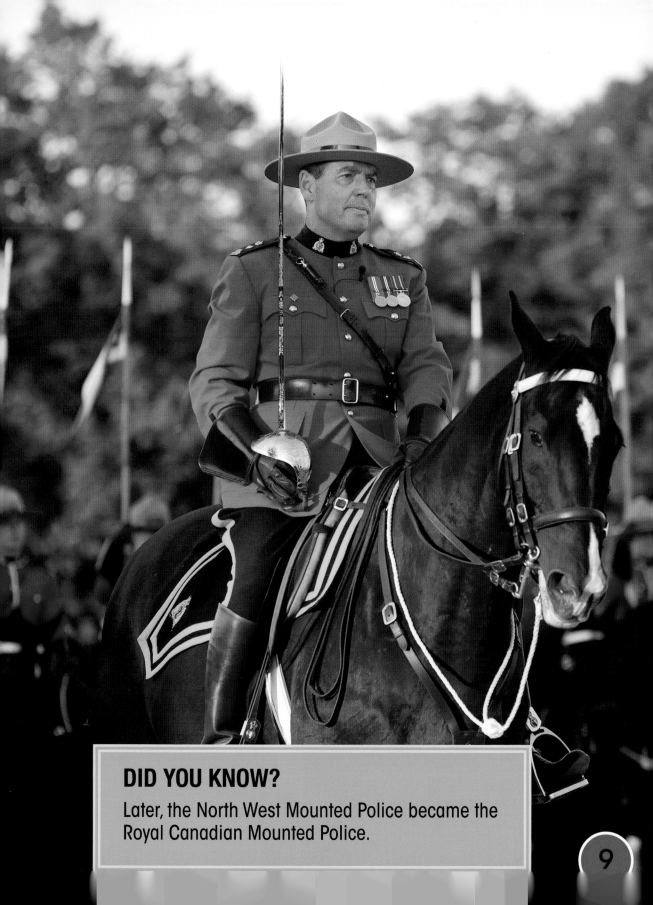

DID YOU KNOW?

Later, the North West Mounted Police became the Royal Canadian Mounted Police.

The bison

On the prairies, many **First Nations** hunted bison. Bison provided them with food and clothing. No part of the bison was wasted. **Tipis** were partly made from bison hides and tools were made from bones. **Settlers** brought horses, guns, and railways to the prairies. They shot and killed the bison in large numbers.

In the early 1800s, there were about 30 million wild bison in Canada.

Settlers wasted most parts of each bison. By 1880, the huge herds on the plains were gone.

Gold!

During the 1850s and 1860s, gold was found in British Columbia. Some people went there to find gold. In 1896, gold was found in the Yukon. About 100,000 people arrived to find gold. They had to climb the Chilkoot Pass to get to the gold fields.

The police made sure each man had supplies for one year before he could climb the Pass.

DID YOU KNOW?
Sometimes it took people months to travel to the gold fields.

A new territory

A town called Dawson City was built near the gold fields. The government wanted to stop this area from becoming part of the United States. This was because gold was worth so much money. In 1898, the government created the Yukon Territory. A railway was built to the gold fields.

Stores, hotels, and gambling halls in Dawson City got very busy. Many people spent their gold when they found it.

The Klondike Mines Railway travelled from Dawson City to the gold fields. The trains carried people, mail, supplies, and gold to and from the mines.

Finding new settlers

Many men visited the west for gold. However, the government wanted whole families to move west and stay. From 1896 onwards, the government **advertised** for **settlers**. They said there would be farms and jobs.

Settlers came from other parts of Canada, the United States, and Europe. They spoke many languages.

Daily life

New **settlers** were called homesteaders. Each homesteader was given 65 hectares of land if they promised to live there. They were asked to build a house and barn in three years. But farming was not easy. Homesteaders had to dig through the tough prairie grass to plant crops.

Families travelled long distances to get to their new farms.

DID YOU KNOW?

The first homes were built of sod: the prairie grass the farmers dug up. Later farmers built wooden houses and barns.

Wheat was the main prairie crop. It was sold to other parts of Canada and the world. It was used to make flour. Soon, the prairies were covered in wheat farms.

Prairie summers were often hot and dry. Homesteaders had to plough **fire breaks** around their fields. These kept homes safe from prairie fires caused by the heat.

Prairie fires could quickly sweep through large parts of prairie land.

DID YOU KNOW?

Some settlers in the west became ranchers and cowhands instead of homesteaders.

Homesteaders planted gardens and raised animals for food. They also grew crops to feed their animals. Some homesteaders could not grow enough food to survive. Sometimes the men would leave to find work. Women and children would stay to work on the farms.

Prairie towns were built along the railway. Stores, schools, restaurants, and churches were built there.

DID YOU KNOW?
Grain elevators stored the wheat crops.

After 1900, more cities were built in Canada. For example, prairie cities were built near the railway lines. This made it easier to move people, **goods**, and crops around the country. Cities had electric lights, streetcars, and exciting things to do.

Many **immigrants** moved to cities because there were jobs in factories and shops.

M. W. & Co. Scales.

42287 The Montgomery Ward Co. Platform Counter Scales, steel bearings, tin scoop, brass beam; weighing ½ oz. to 240 lbs. Warranted reliable (See cut). Weight, boxed for shipment, 39 lbs. Price, each.................................$2.43

42288 The House-keeper's Friend, price with plat-form, no scoop; shipping weight 15 lbs. Weighs from ½ oz. to 25 lbs. Each...........................$1.68
42289 With tin scoop. Each.........................2.00
Our scales are all packed ready for shipment. We have some of these scales, which have been in constant use for several years, and they answer our purpose as well as those sold for $14.

Garden Trowels.

42292 Garden Trowels: extra quality, cast steel; made in four sizes.

Length, inches	.5	6	7	8
Price, each	$0.04	$0.05	$0.06	$0.07
Price, per dozen	.44	.54	.65	.75

Weeding Hooks.

42294 Weeding Hook, wood handle, entire length, including handle, 10 in. This pattern is the most popular style of hand weeder; each.........................$0.07
Per dozen.................................. .75

Strawberry Forks.

42296 Strawberry Forks. Japanned iron fork wood handle, length, including handle, 11 in. Made in two patterns, light and heavy.
Light pattern, each.....$0.08 Per dozen $0.87
Heavy pattern, each.....12 Per dozen.... 1.30

Garden Line Reel.

42299 Garden Line Reel. Malleable iron, japanned; no line furnished with reel. Each.....$0.37
Per dozen.................................. 4.00
42304 Garden Rake and Hoe combined, very nice for weeding purposes 4 and 6 teeth. Polished steel.
4 teeth. Each, $0.25
Per doz............$2.70
6 teeth. Each, $0.35
Per doz............$3.85
42305 Garden Rake and Hoe combined, malleable iron, cast steel blade, 4 and 6 teeth.
4 teeth. Each.................$0.18
Per dozen.................. 1.95
6 teeth. Each................. .20
Per dozen.................. 2.16

Scuffle Hoe.

42307 Scuffle Hoe, malleable socket, steel blade, 6 foot handle. Each..$0.40
Per dozen.................. 4 25

Onion Hoe.

42310 Onion Hoe, polished, solid shank; a very convenient shape.
Each. $0.25
Per doz. 2.70

Hoes.

42313 Garden Socket Hoes, blued.
Each.................................$0.30
Per dozen.................. 3.00
42314 Garden Shank Hoes, blued. Each......... .25
Per dozen.................. 2.75
42315 Warren Garden Hoes, extra cast steel, polished. Garden size. Each.................. .40
Per dozen.................. 4.55
Field sizes. Each .... .50
Per dozen.................. 5 40

Garden Rakes.

42320 Garden Rake, malleable iron, polished, 12 teeth. Each.................................$0.20
Per dozen.................. 2.15
42321 Garden Rake, cast steel polished, 12 teeth.
Each.................. .35
Per dozen.................. 3.55
42322 14 teeth Garden Rake, cast steel. Each.... .40
Per dozen.................. 3.90

Garden Rakes—Continued.

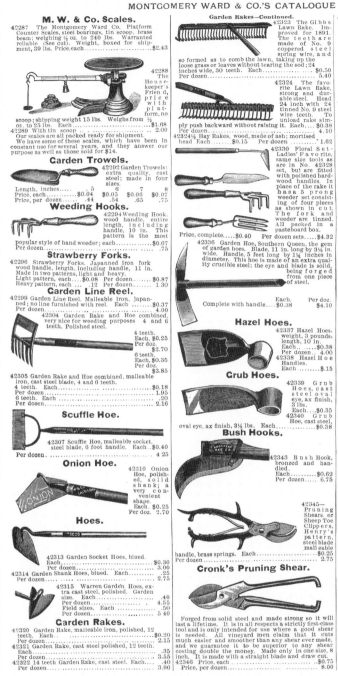

42323 The Gibbs Lawn Rake. Improved for 1891. The teeth are made of No. 9 coppered steel spring wire, and so formed as to comb the lawn, taking up the loose grass or leaves without tearing the sod; 24 inches wide, 30 teeth. Each...........$0.50
Per dozen.................. 5.40
42324 The favorite Lawn Rake, strong and durable steel. Head 24 inch with 24 tinned No. 9 steel wire teeth. To unload rake simply push backward without raising it. Each.. $0.38
Per dozen.................. 4.10
42324½ Hay Rakes, wood, made of ash; mortised head. Each.....$0.15 Per dozen.......1.62
42330 Floral Set. Ladies' Favorite, same size tools as are in No. 42328 set, but are fitted with polished hardwood handles. In place of the rake it has a 5 prong weeder set consisting of four pieces as shown in cut. The fork and weeder are tinned. All packed in a pasteboard box.
Price, complete....$0.40 Per dozen sets....$4.32
42336 Garden Hoe, Southern Queen, the gem of garden hoes. Blade, 11 in. long by 3½ in. wide. Handle, 5 feet long by 1¼ inches in diameter. This hoe is made of an extra quality crucible steel; the eye and blade is solid, being forged from one piece of steel.

Each. Per doz.
Complete with handle...$0.38 $4.10

Hazel Hoes.

42337 Hazel Hoes, weight, 3 pounds, length, 10 in.
Each.............$0.38
Per dozen.... 4.00
42338 Hazel Hoe Handles.
Each ....$.15

Grub Hoes.

42339 Grub Hoes, cast steel oval eye, ax finish, 3 lbs.
Each.......$0.35
42340 Grub Hoe, cast steel, oval eye, ax finish, 3½ lbs. Each.........$0.38

Bush Hooks.

42343 Bush Hook, bronzed and handled.
Each...........$0.62
Per dozen.... 6.75

42345— Pruning Shears, or Sheep Toe Clippers, Henry's pattern, steel blade malleable handle, brass springs. Each.......................$0.25
Per dozen.................. 2.75

Cronk's Pruning Shear.

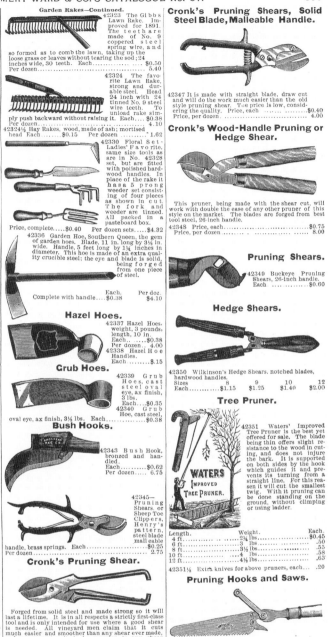

Forged from solid steel and made strong so it will last a lifetime. It is in all respects a strictly first-class tool and is only intended for use where a good shear is needed. All vineyard men claim that it cuts much easier and smoother than any shear ever made, and we guarantee it to be superior to any shear costing double the money. Made only in one size, 8 inch. It is made with a straight blade and draw cut.
42346 Price, each $0.75
Price, per dozen.................. 8.00

Cronk's Pruning Shears, Solid Steel Blade, Malleable Handle.

42347 It is made with straight blade, draw cut and will do the work much easier than the old style pruning shear. The price is low, considering the quality. Price, each $0.40
Price, per dozen.................. 4.00

Cronk's Wood-Handle Pruning or Hedge Shear.

This pruner, being made with the shear cut, will work with double the ease of any other pruner of this style on the market. The blades are forged from best tool steel, 26-inch handle.
42348 Price, each.................................$0.75
Price, per dozen.................. 8.00

Pruning Shears.

42349 Buckeye Pruning Shears, 26-inch blade.
Each $0.60

Hedge Shears.

42350 Wilkinson's Hedge Shears, notched blades, hardwood handles.

Sizes	8	9	10	12
Each	$1.15	$1.25	$1.40	$2.00

Tree Pruner.

42351 Waters' Improved Tree Pruner is the best yet offered for sale. The blade being thin offers slight resistance to the wood in cutting, and does not injure the bark. It is supported on both sides by the hook which guides it and prevents its turning from a straight line. For this reason it will cut the smallest twig. With it pruning can be done standing on the ground, without climbing or using ladder.

WATERS IMPROVED TREE PRUNER.

Length.	Weight.	Each.
4 ft	2¼ lbs	$0.45
6 ft	.3 lbs	.50
8 ft	3½ lbs	.55
10 ft	.4 lbs	.58
12 ft	4½ lbs	.63

42351½ Extra knives for above pruners, each... .20

Pruning Hooks and Saws.

42352 Disston's Pruning Hook and Saw; can be used with or without pole; the saw can be detached when the hook alone is to be used.
Each, without pole.................................$1.20

A changing country

Canada changed a lot in the 1900s. Canada slowly moved towards **independence** from Great Britain. The role of women changed, too. During World War I (1914–1918), women were allowed to vote for the first time. Soon, women felt they should help run the country and do the same jobs as men.

Thousands of men left their homes to fight in Europe.

Making bannock

Scottish traders brought Bannock recipes to Canada. Aboriginal people and prairie families made it. Ask an adult to help you make this.

Ingredients:

4 cups whole-wheat flour
4 tbsp baking powder
1 tsp salt
4 tbsp fat such as lard, suet, butter, or margarine
2 cups water

What to do:

1. Preheat the oven to 425°F.
2. Grease a 9 x 13 inch cake pan.
3. Mix together the flour, baking powder, and salt.
4. Cut the fat into the flour mixture until there are lumps the size of peas.
5. Make a hole in the middle of the flour. Pour the water in the hole. Mix gently. It will make very sticky dough.
6. Put the dough in the greased pan.
7. Bake for about 30-40 minutes, until the top is golden. Check it is cooked by putting a toothpick or knife in the middle. No dough should stick to it.
8. Cool in the pan for a few minutes. Then, turn it out of the pan onto a rack to finish cooling.

29

Glossary

Aboriginal original and ancestors of the people who live in a land; in Canada, this includes the Inuit and the Métis people

advertise tell lots of people about something

colony area ruled by another country

fire break strip of land where grass or plants have been removed to stop a fire

First Nations people who have lived in Canada for thousands of years; not Inuit or Métis

goods things that are made and sold

grain elevator tall building for storing grain

immigrant person who moves to a new country

independence free from another person or group's control

province section of the country with its own government, whose power is granted by the Constitution Act

settlers people who build and stay somewhere

territory section of the country with its own local government that is given power by the federal government

tipi prairie First Nations home made out of tall poles wrapped in bison hide

treaty written agreement between two nations

Find out more

Books

The Kids Book of Canadian Immigration Deborah Hodge (Kids Can Press, 2006)

The Mounties, A.G. Smith (Fitzhenry & Whiteside, 2008)

Websites

FactHound offers a safe, fun way to find Internet sites related to this book. All of the sites on FactHound have been researched by our staff.

Here's all you do:

Visit www.facthound.com
Type in this code: 9781410981219

Index